AF481159

PRINTING PRACTICE

Lowercase and Uppercase Letters Edition

Children's Reading and Writing Books

This workbook will help your child practice his or her writing and familiarize them with each Letter of the Alphabet.

Let's learn the Alphabet!

The Alphabet

Aa Bb Cc Dd Ee
Ff Gg Hh Ii Jj Kk
Ll Mm Nn Oo Pp
Qq Rr Ss Tt Uu
Vv Ww Xx Yy Zz

Practice Handwriting

It's time to practice writing the letters.
Are you ready?

Have fun writing!

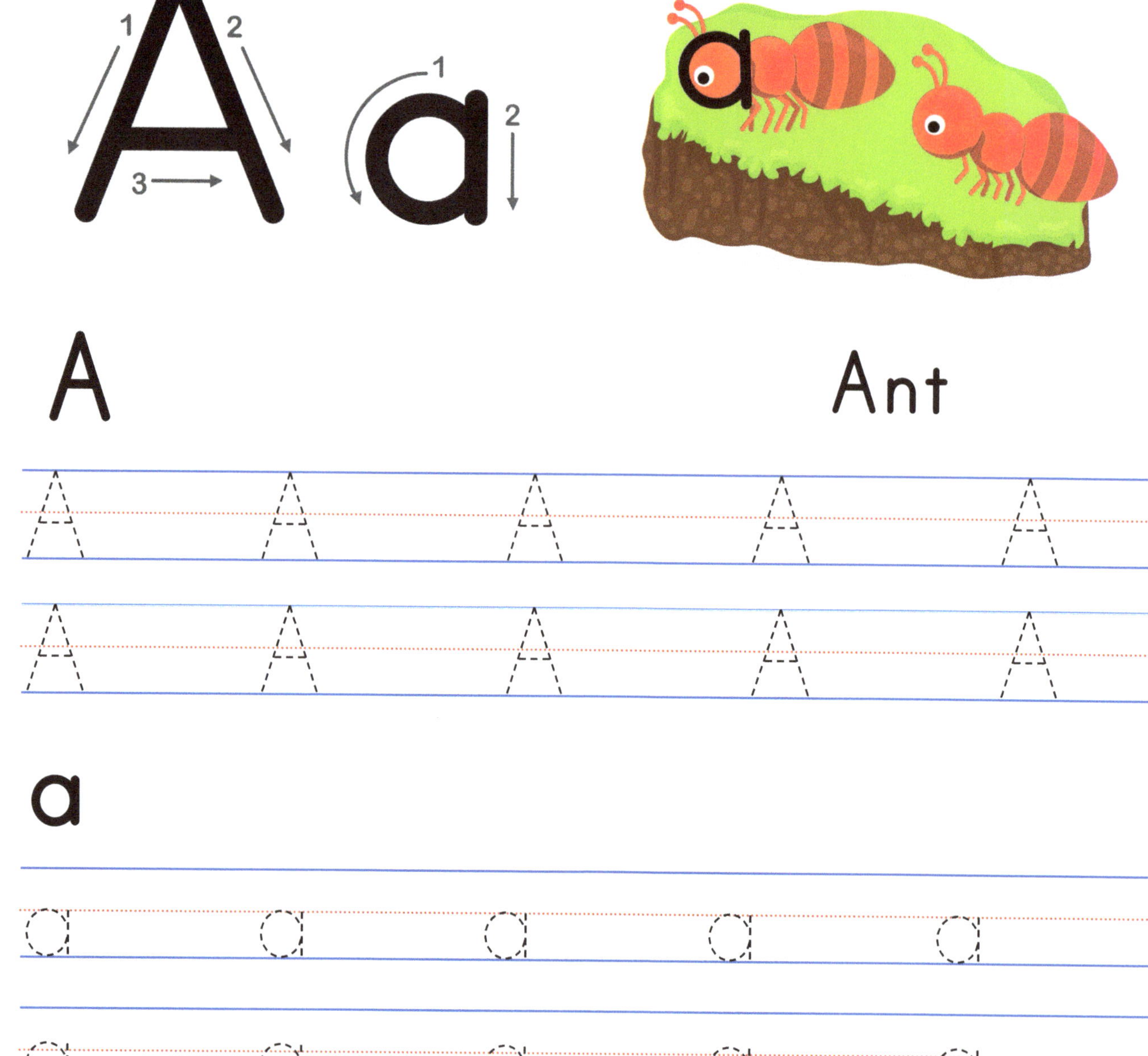
A
a
Ant

Trace the following uppercase and lowercase letters.

B b

Butterfly

B

b

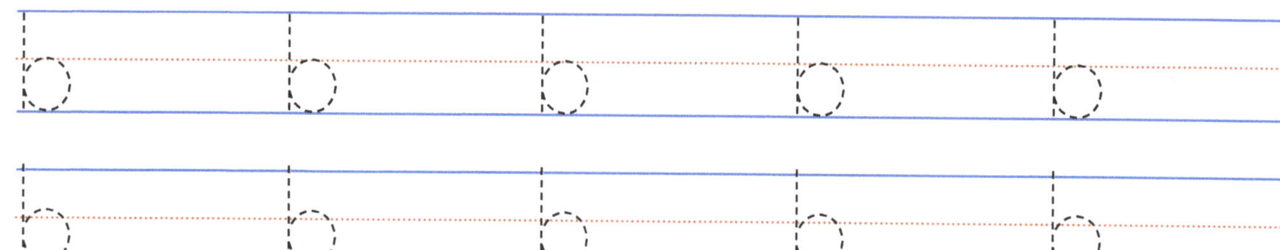

Trace the following uppercase and lowercase letters.

C

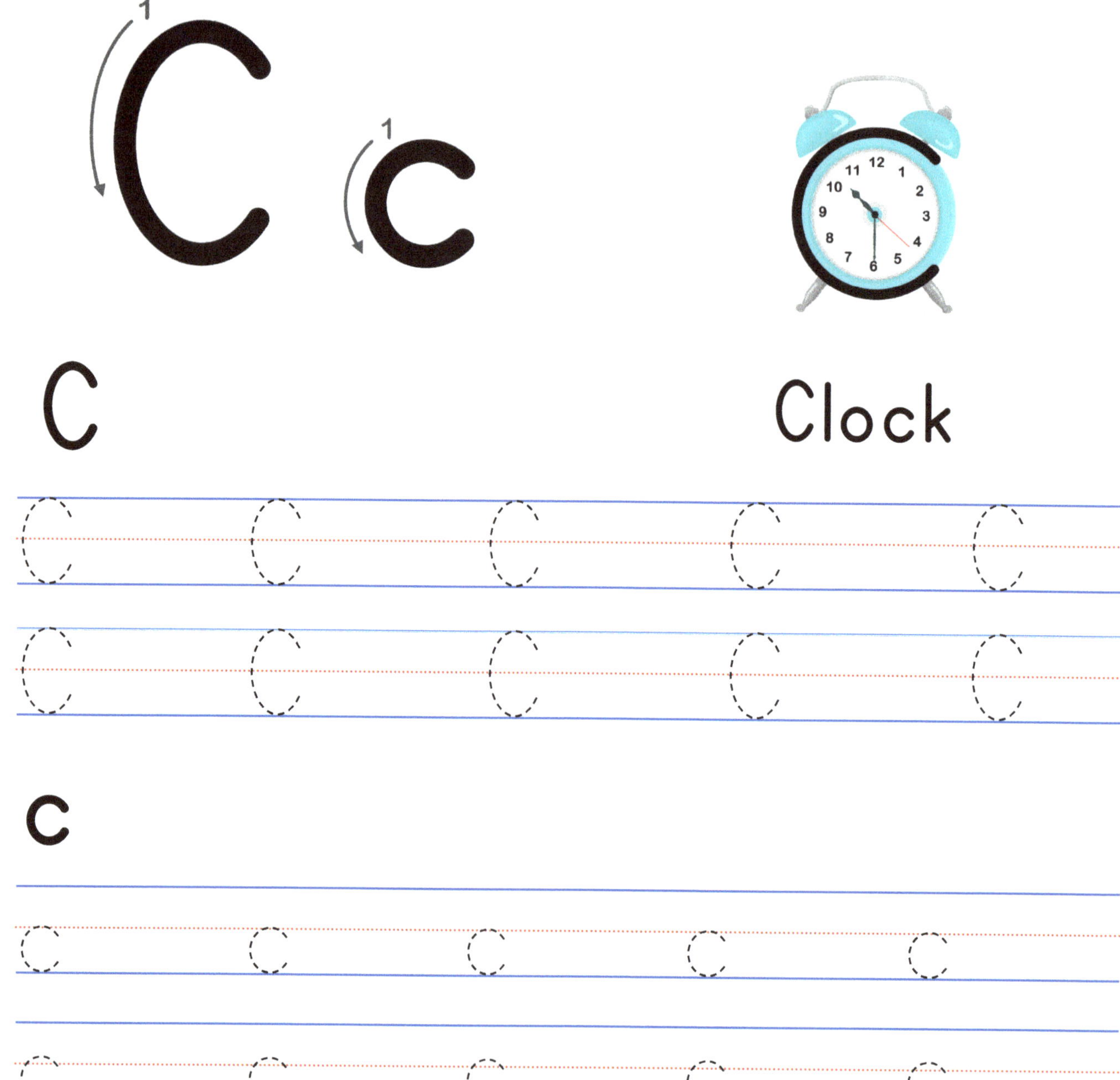

Clock

C

c

Trace the following uppercase and lowercase letters.

D d

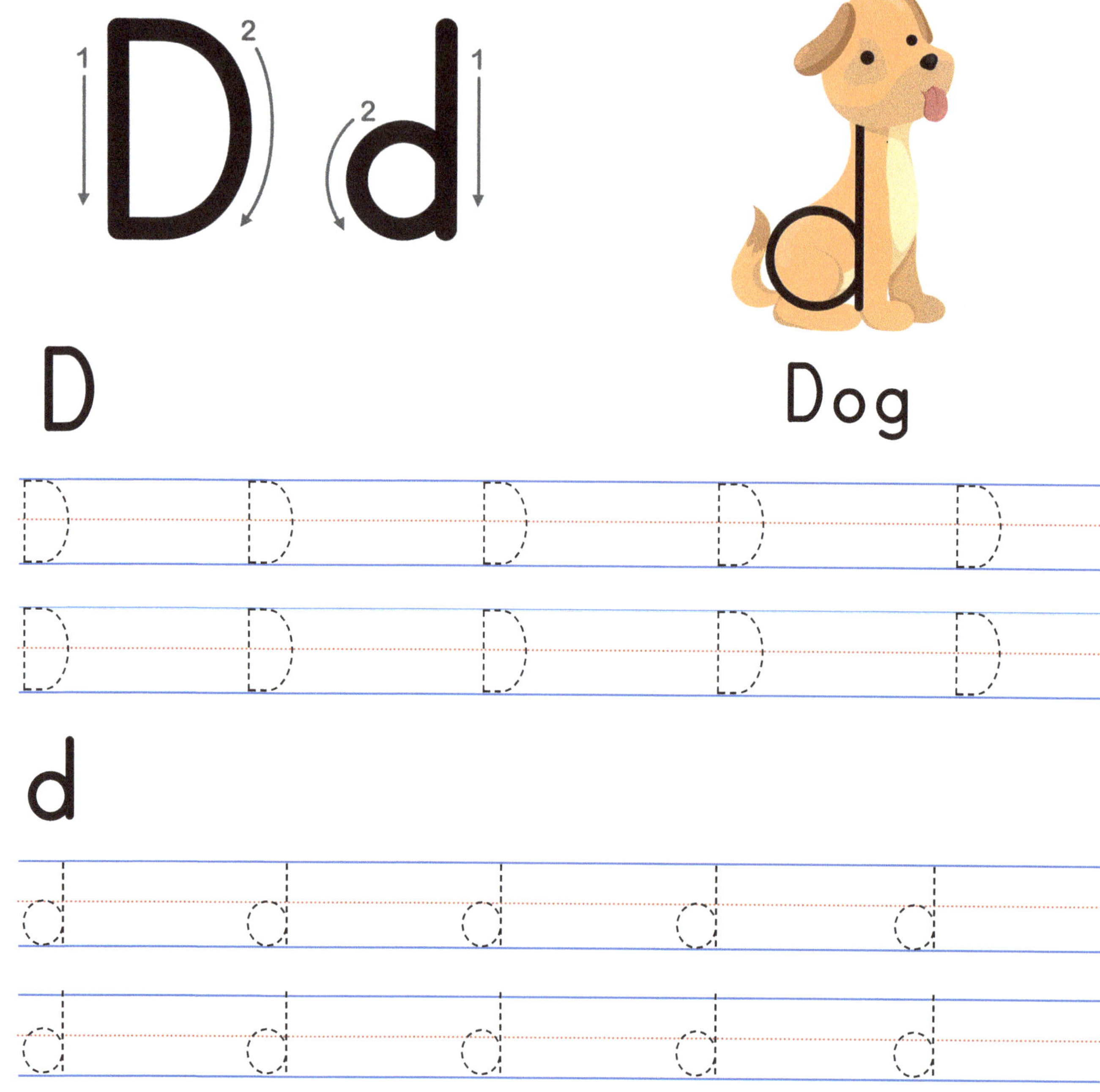

Trace the following uppercase and lowercase letters.

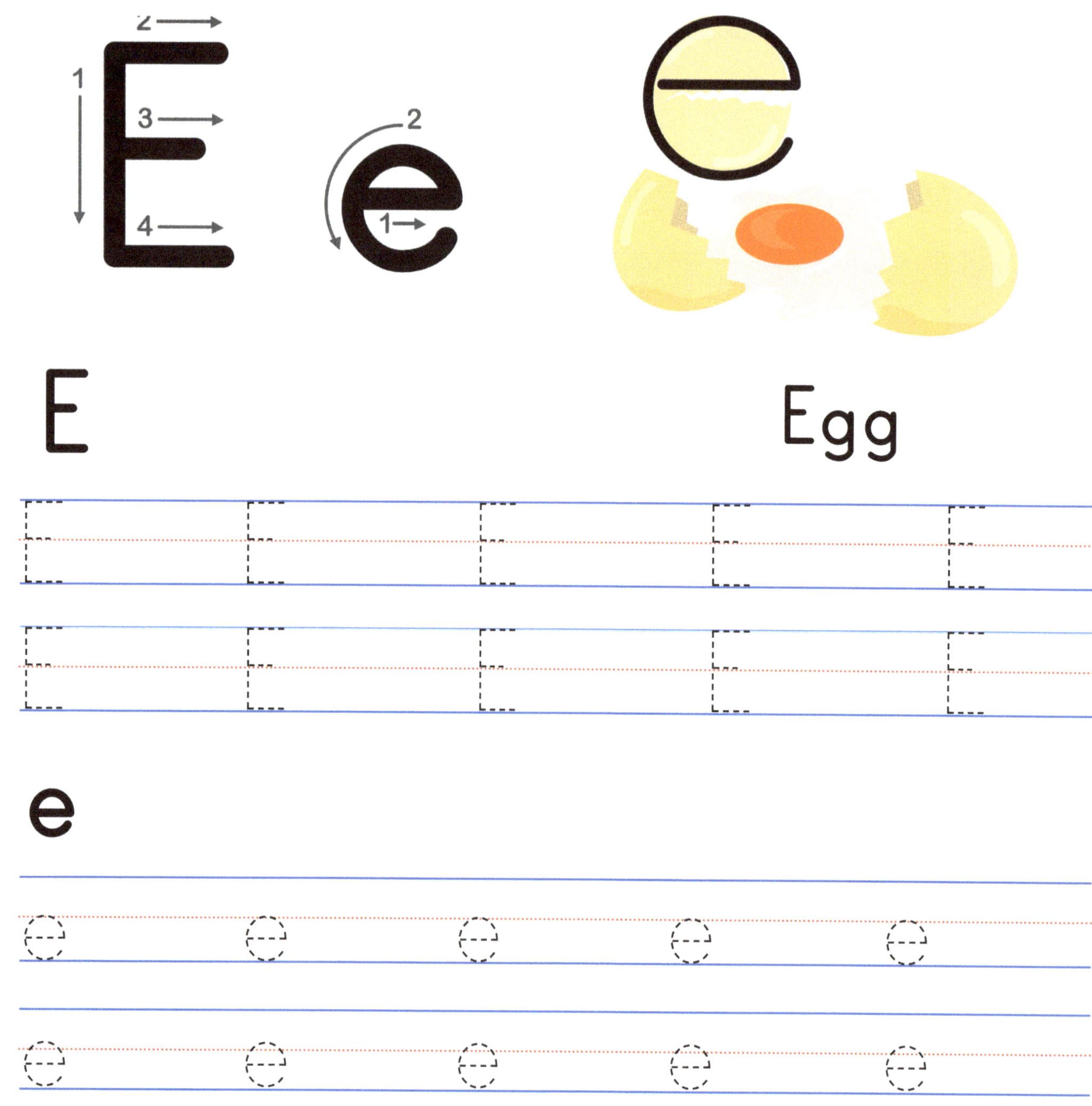

E
e
Egg

Trace the following uppercase and lowercase letters.

2
1
3
1
2
F
Fern
F
f

Trace the following uppercase and lowercase letters.

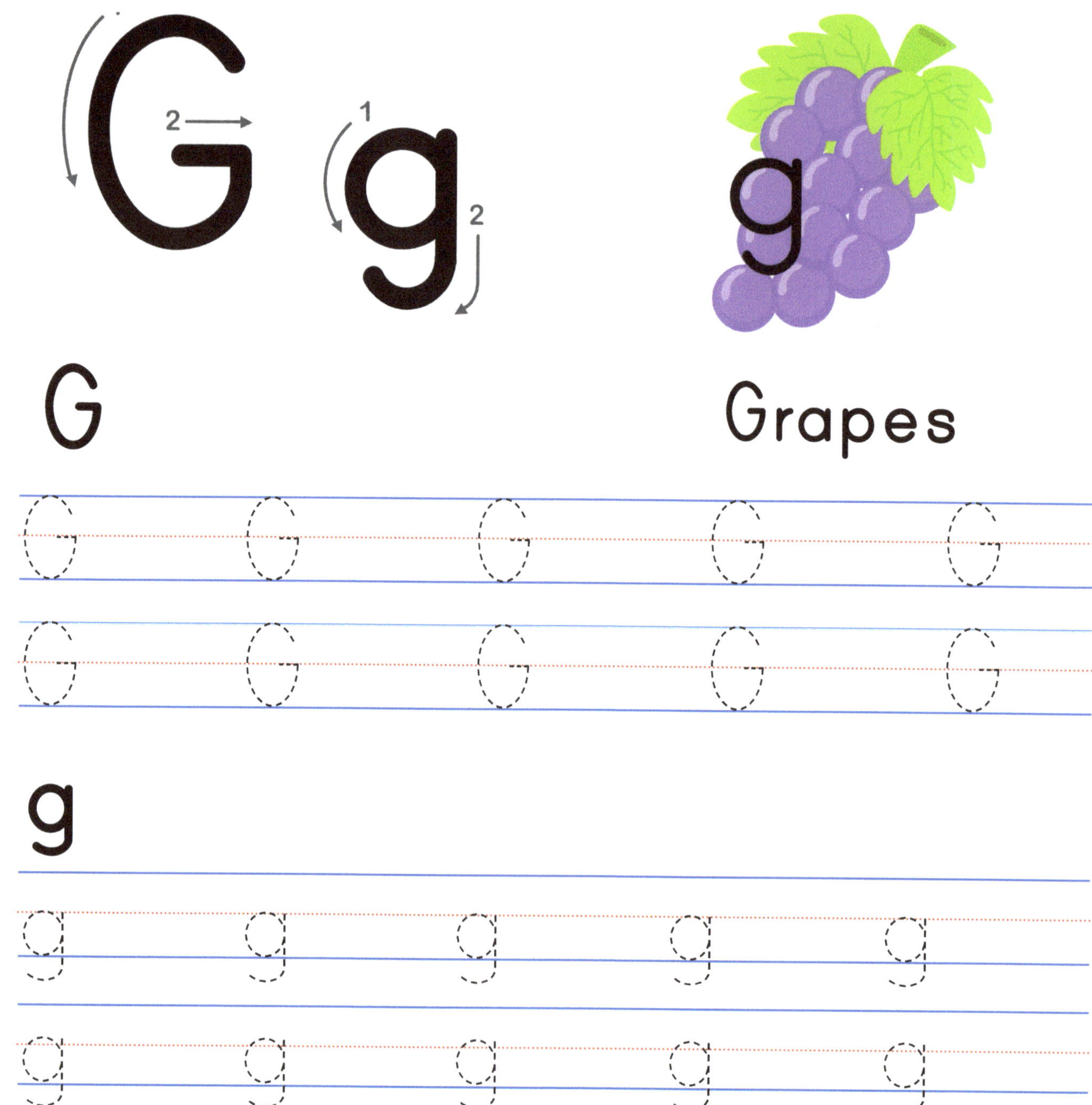

G
g
Grapes

Trace the following uppercase and lowercase letters.

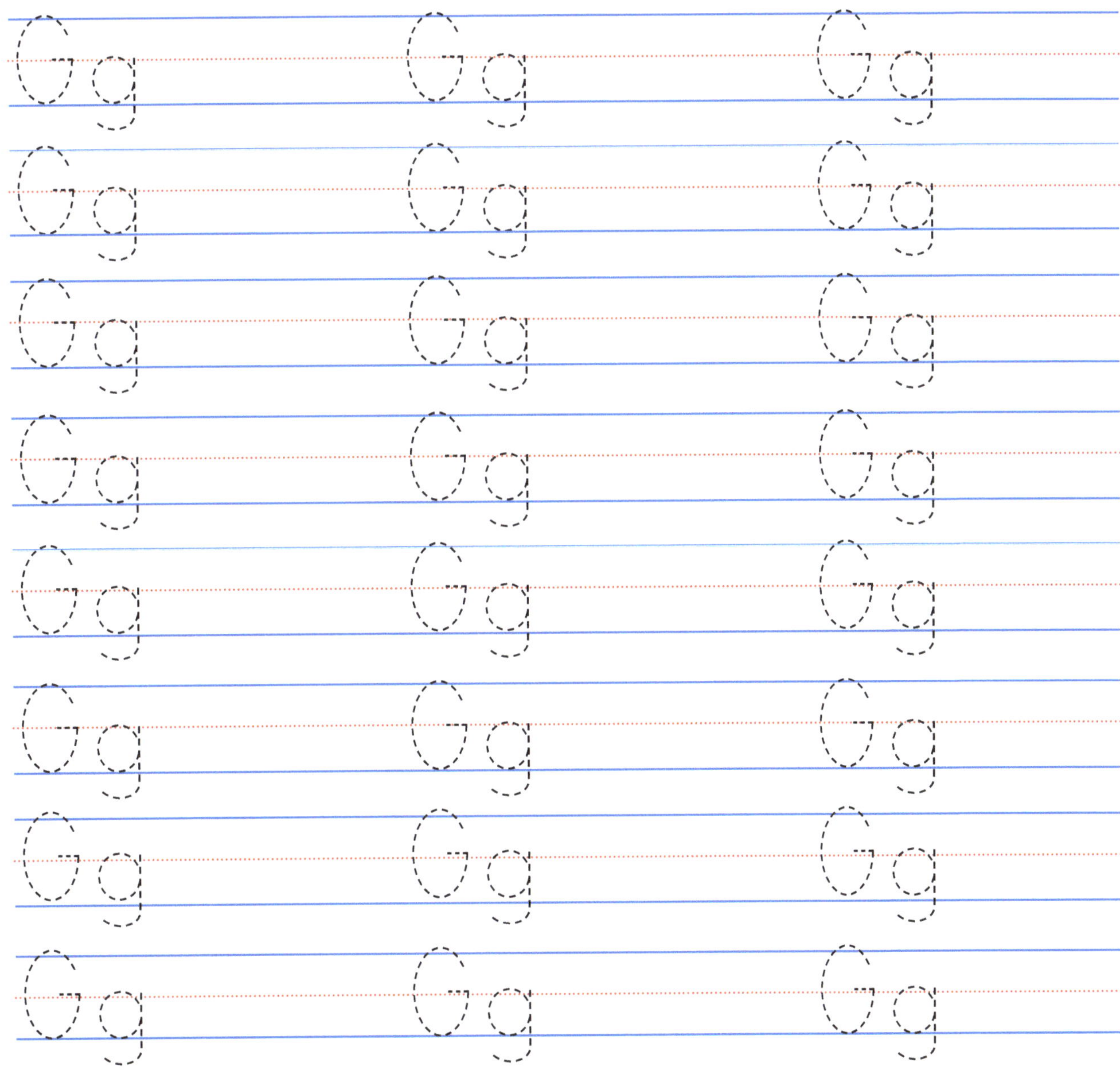

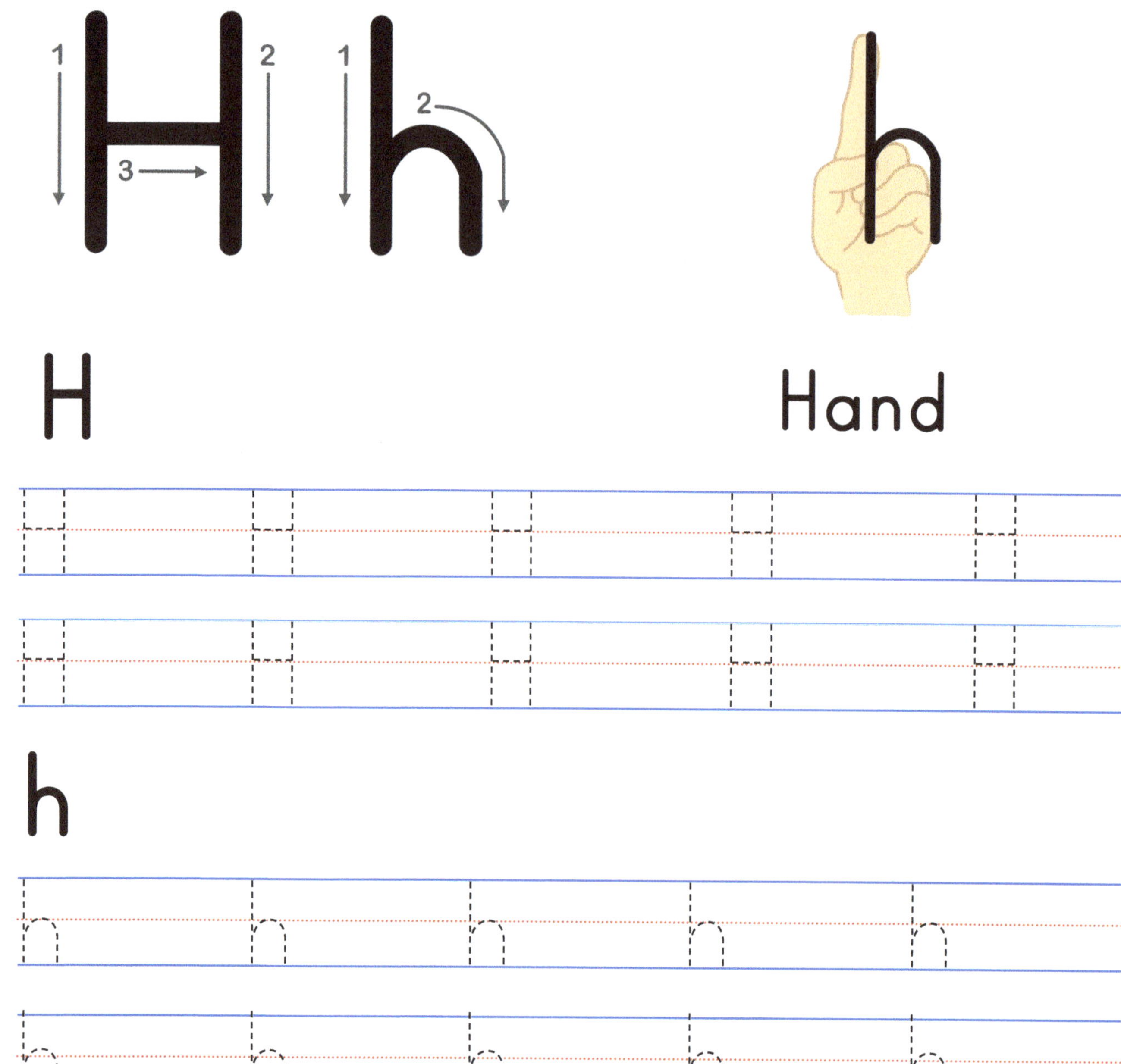

H

Hand

h

Trace the following uppercase and lowercase letters.

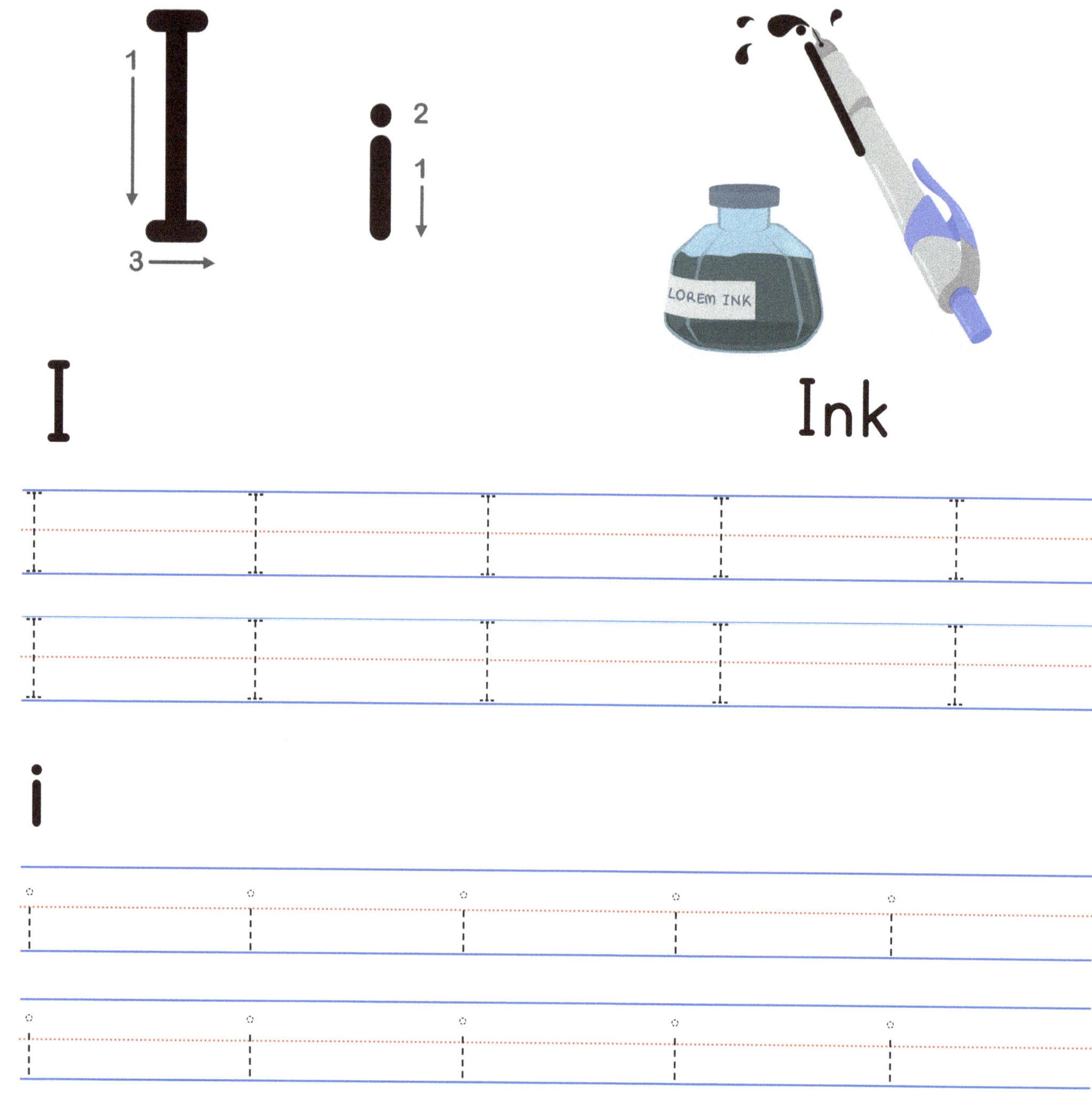
1
2
1
3
LOREM INK
Ink
I
I
i

Trace the following uppercase and lowercase letters.

J

J

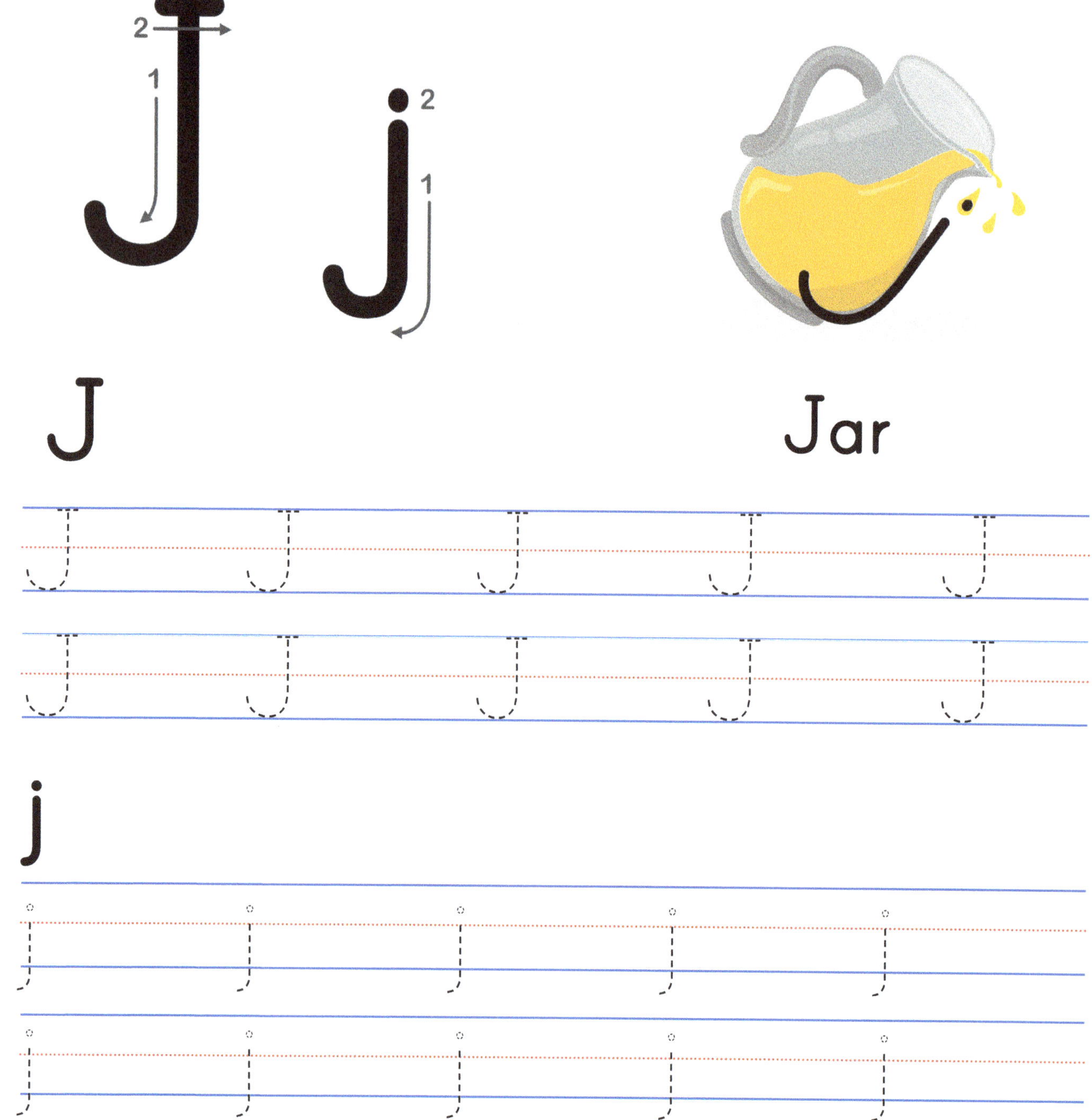

Jar

j

Trace the following uppercase and lowercase letters.

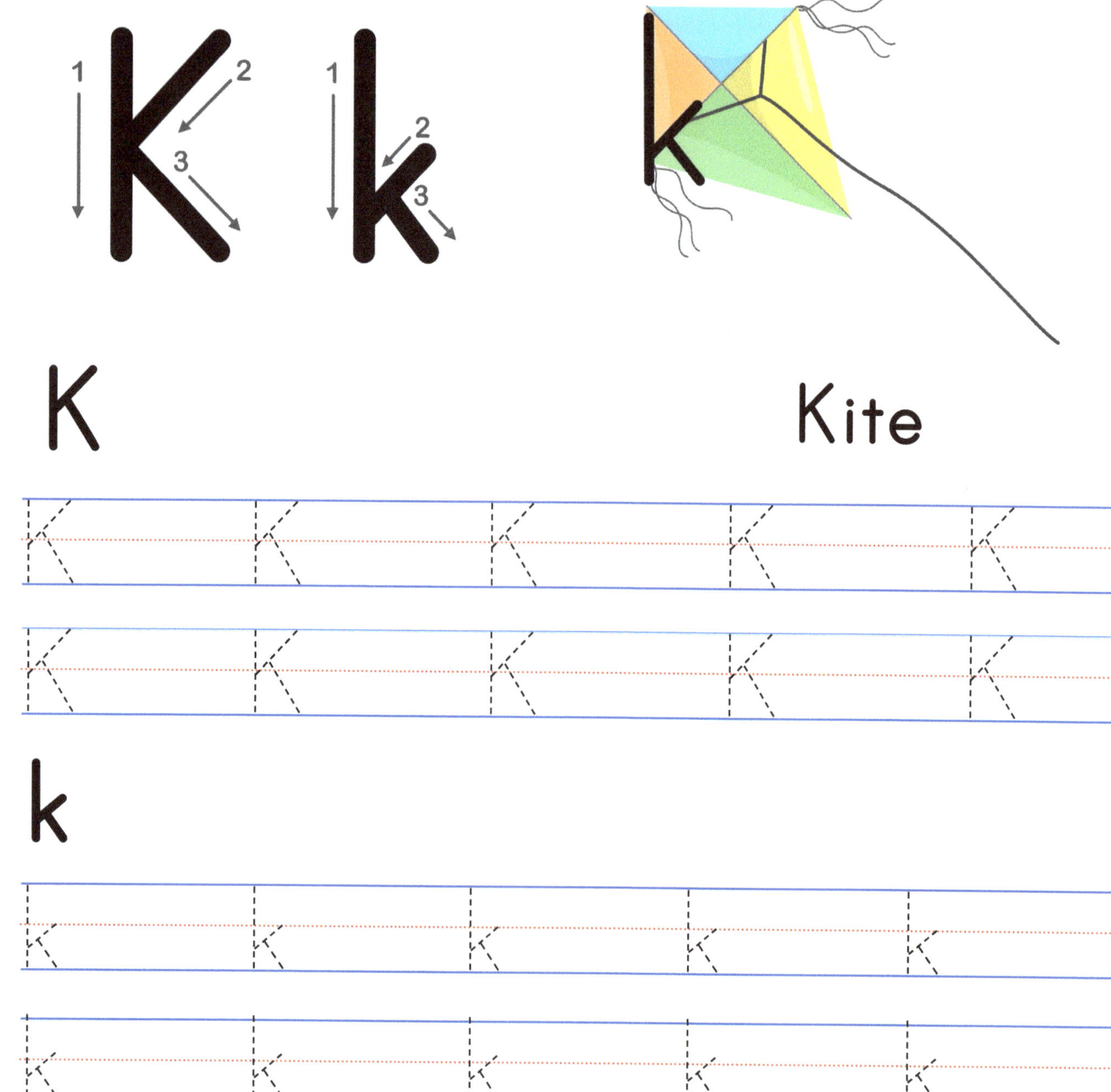

K

Kite

k

Trace the following uppercase and lowercase letters.

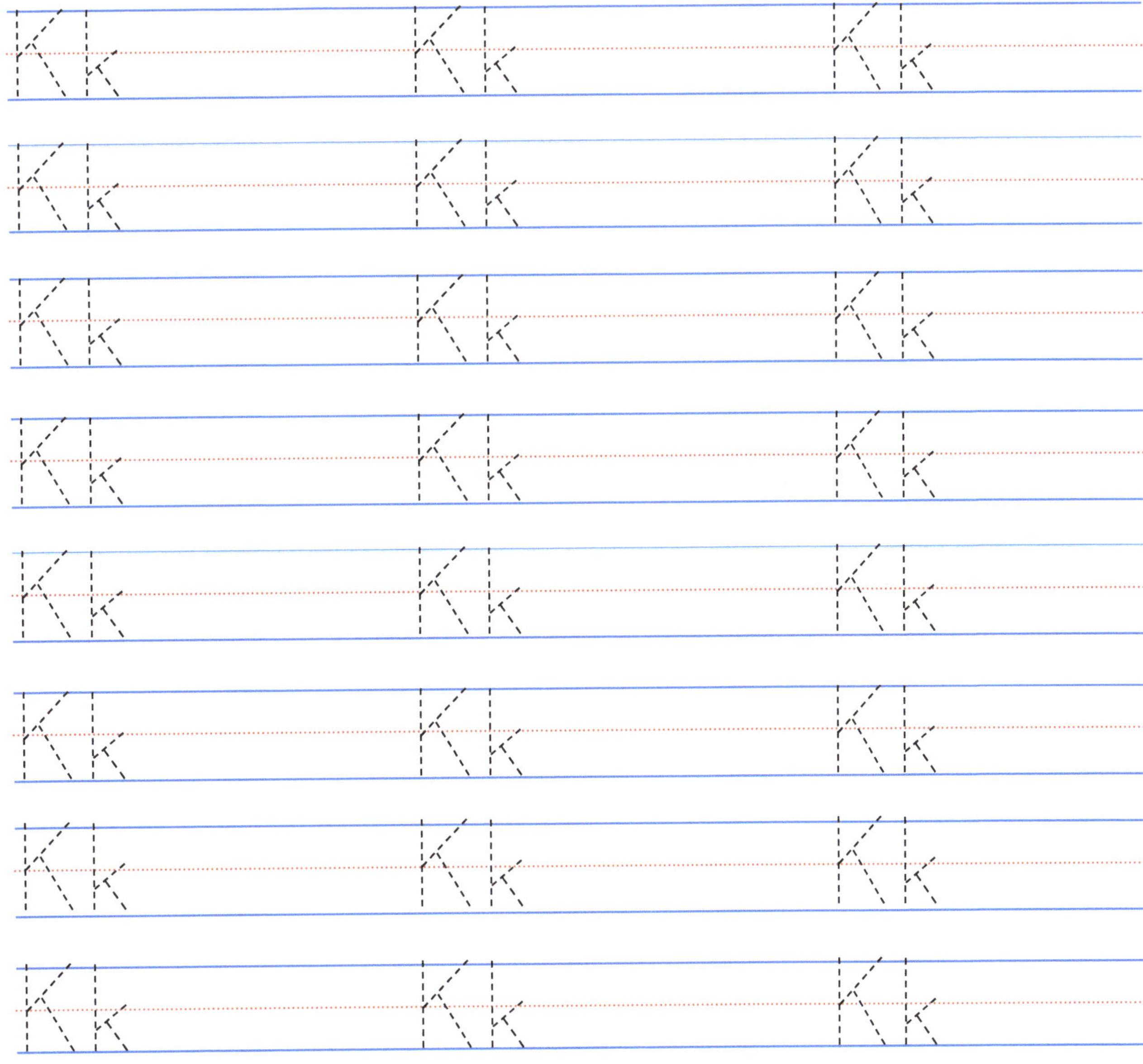

L l

L

Ladybug

L

l

Trace the following uppercase and lowercase letters.

M m

M

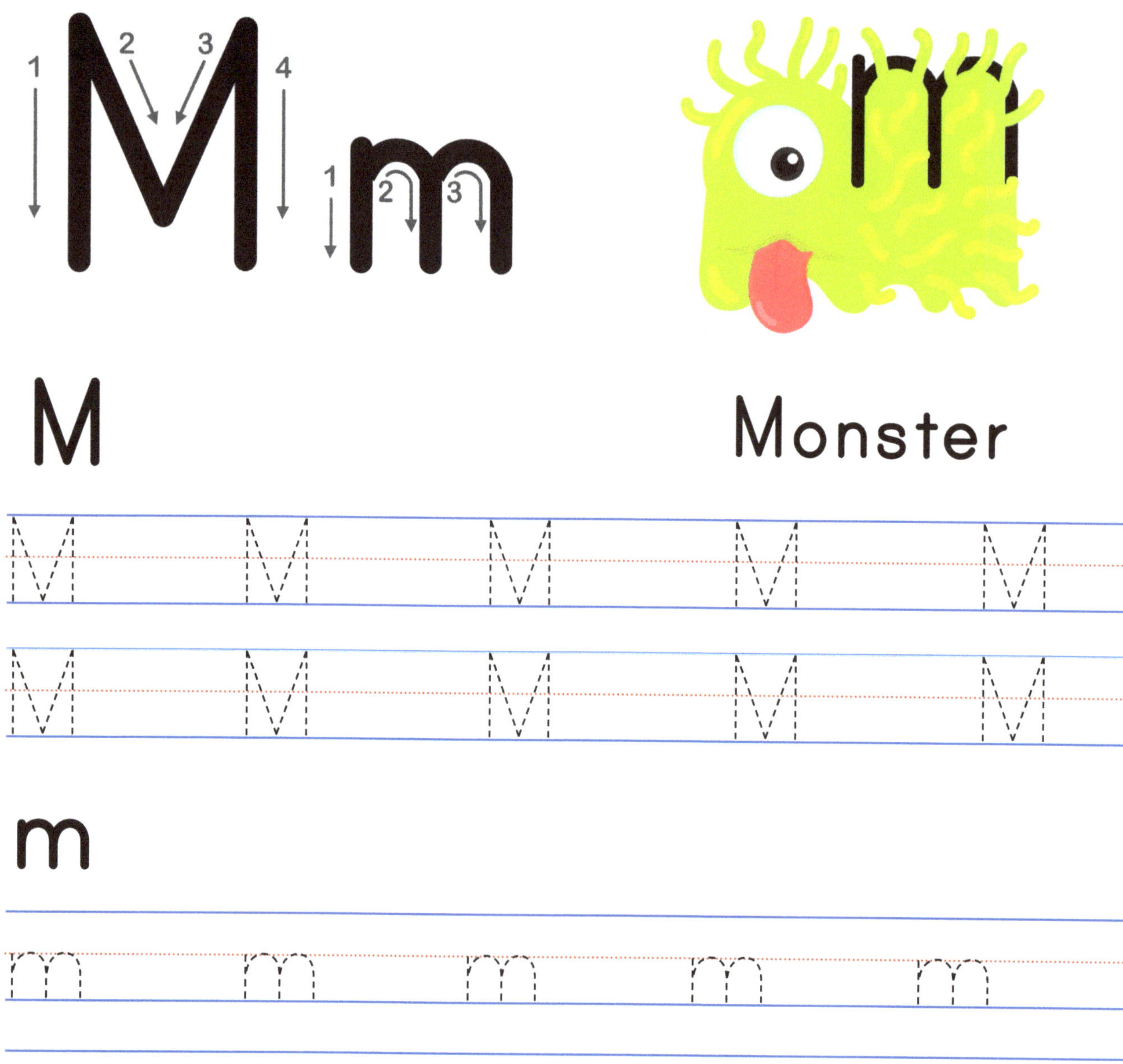

Monster

m

Trace the following uppercase and lowercase letters.

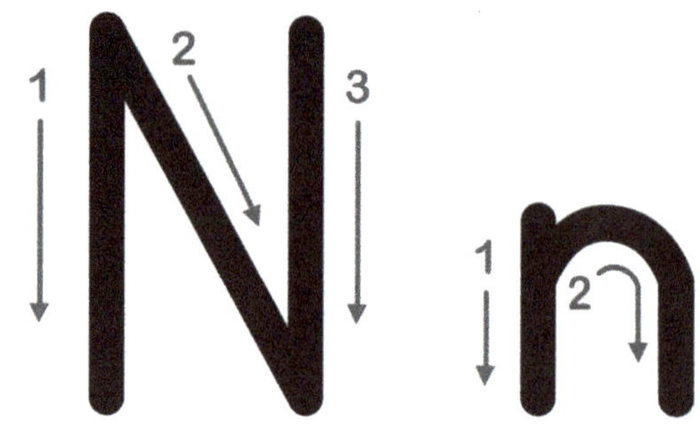

News

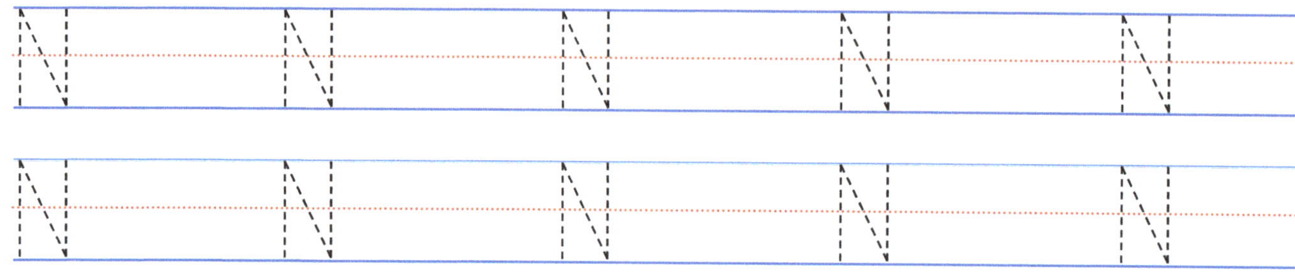

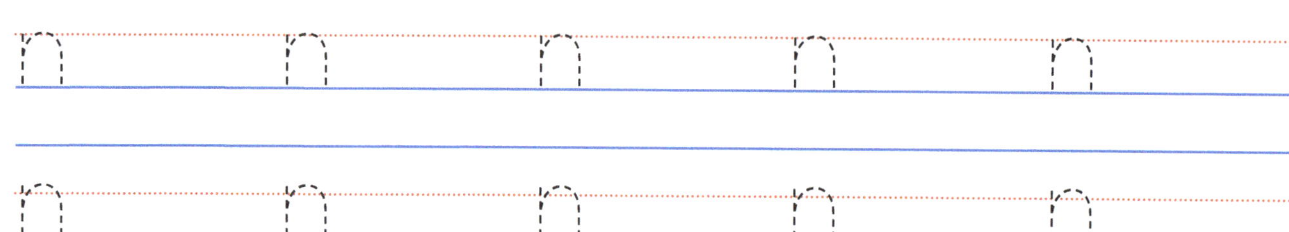

Trace the following uppercase and lowercase letters.

O o

O

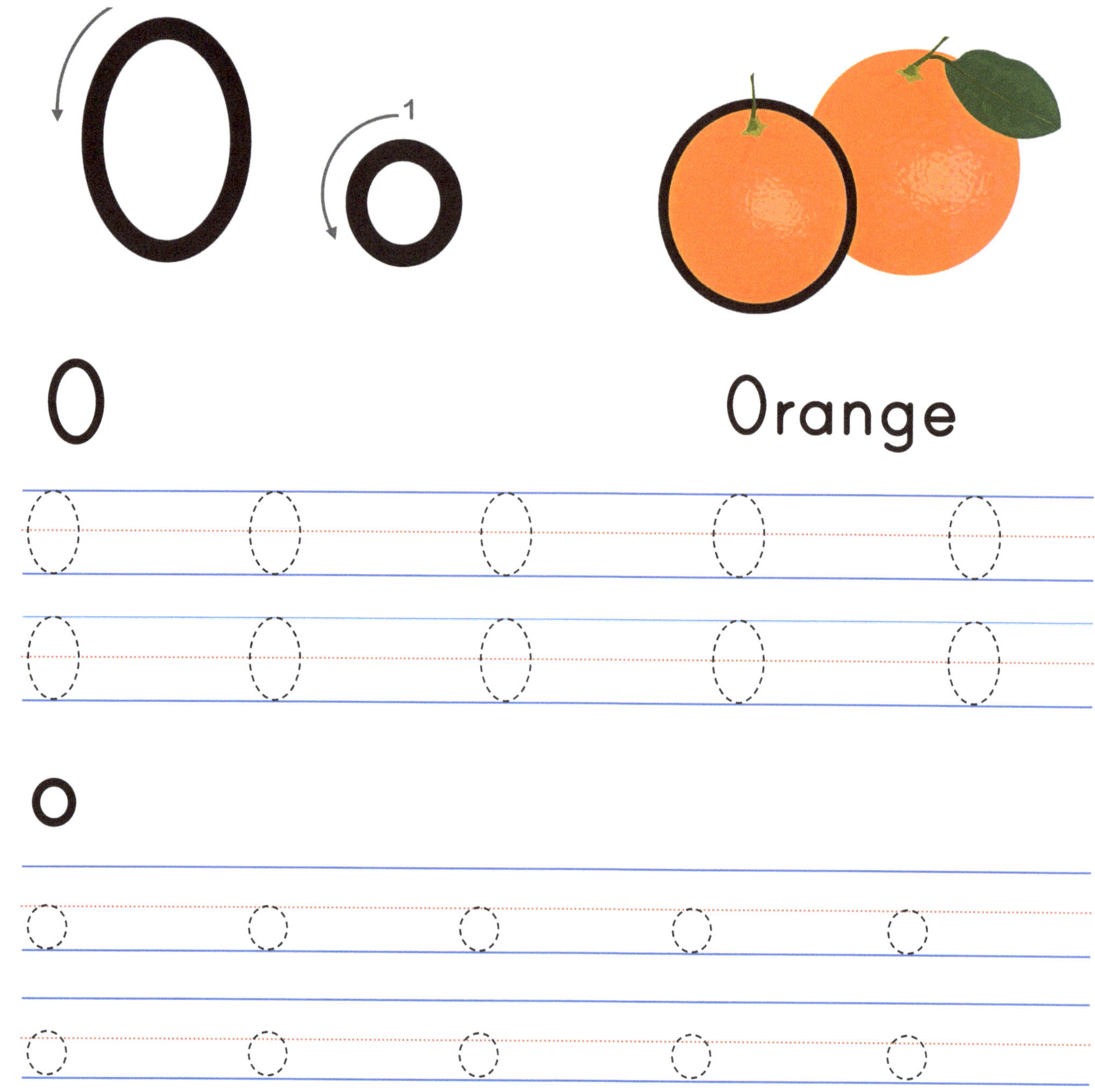

Orange

Trace the following uppercase and lowercase letters.

P

p

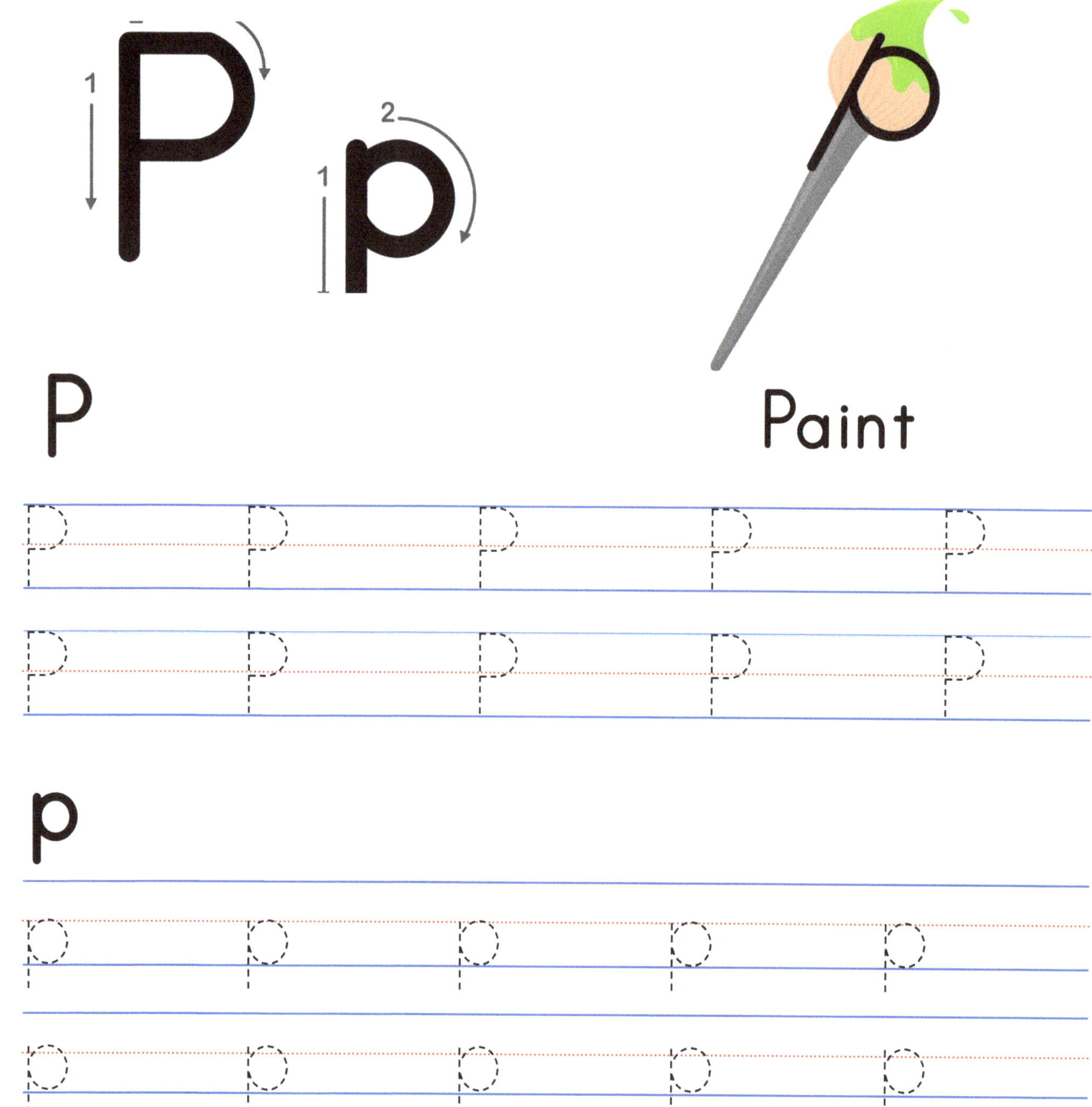

Trace the following uppercase and lowercase letters.

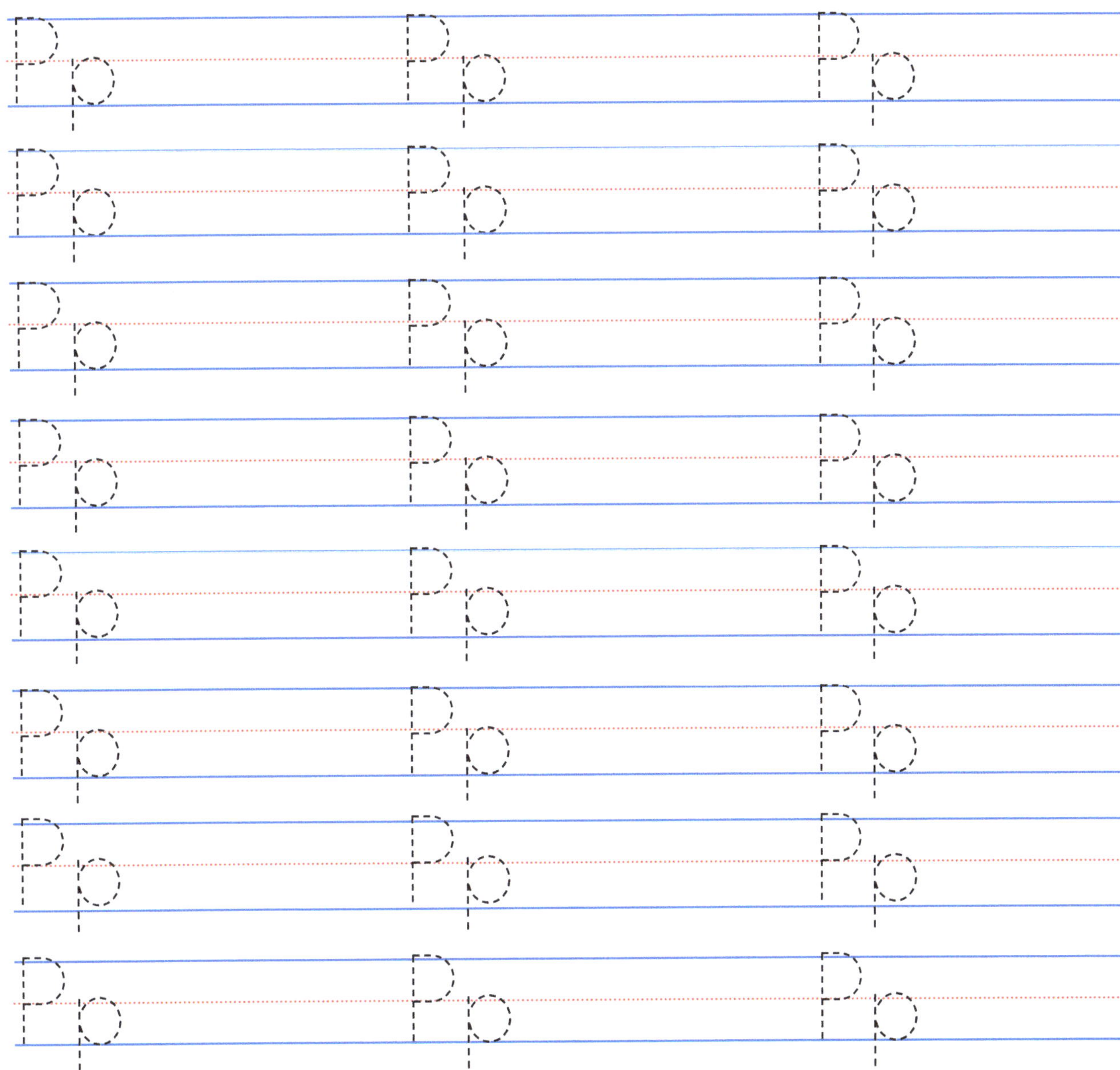

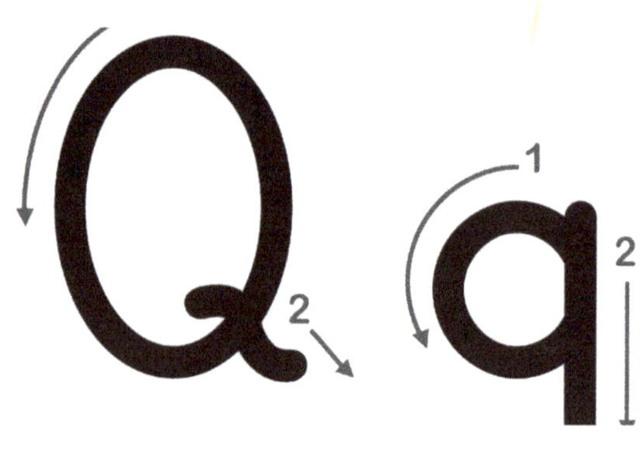

Q

Quilt

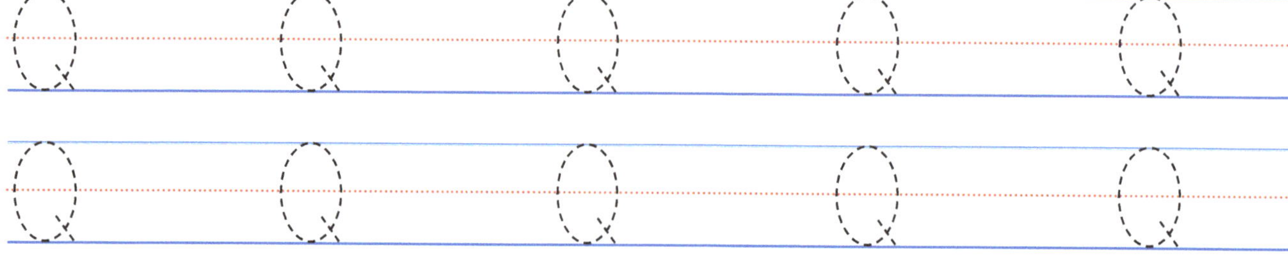

q

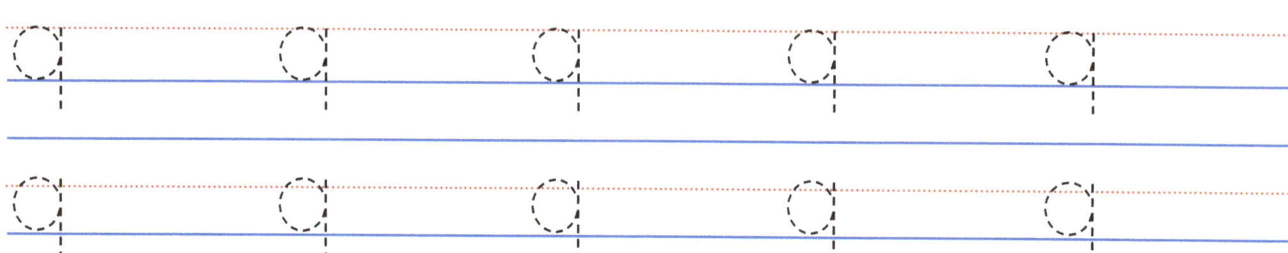

Trace the following uppercase and lowercase letters.

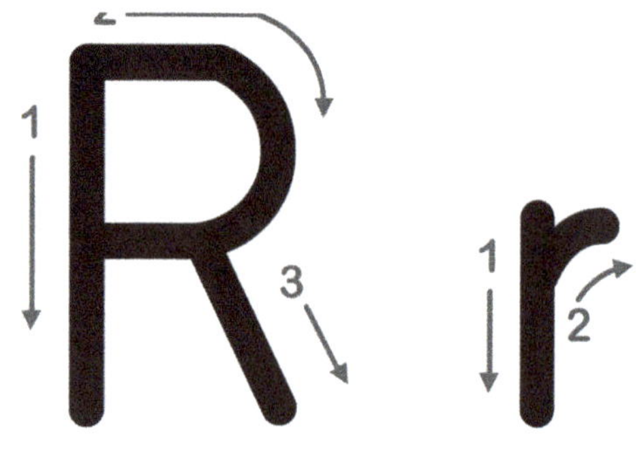

R

Rose

R

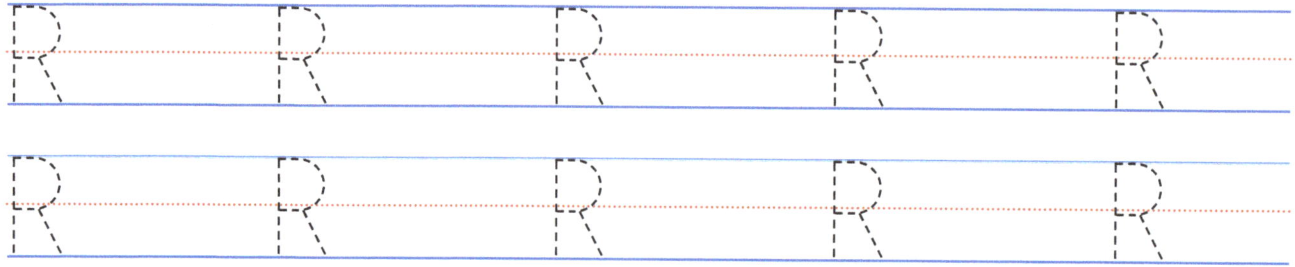

r

Trace the following uppercase and lowercase letters.

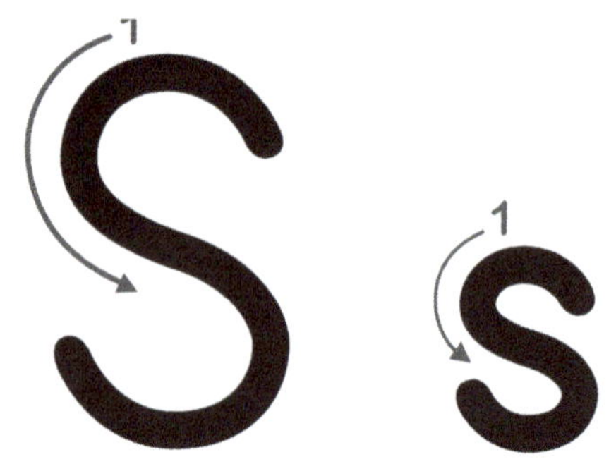

S

Snail

S

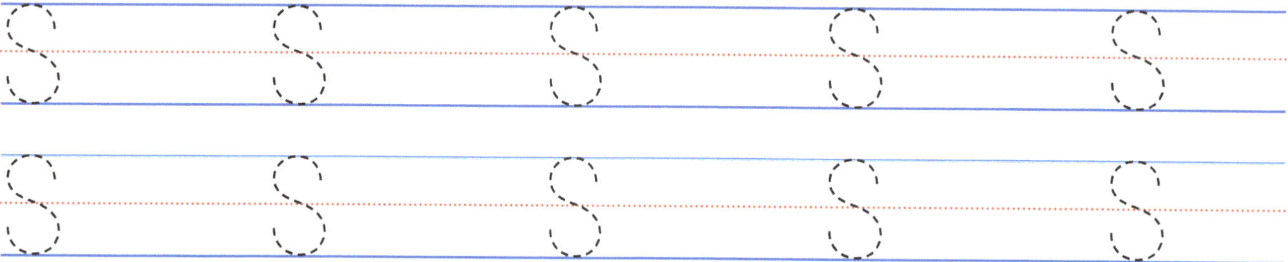

s

Trace the following uppercase and lowercase letters.

T
t
T
Tree
t

Trace the following uppercase and lowercase letters.

U

u

Umbrella

Trace the following uppercase and lowercase letters.

Vegetable

Trace the following uppercase and lowercase letters.

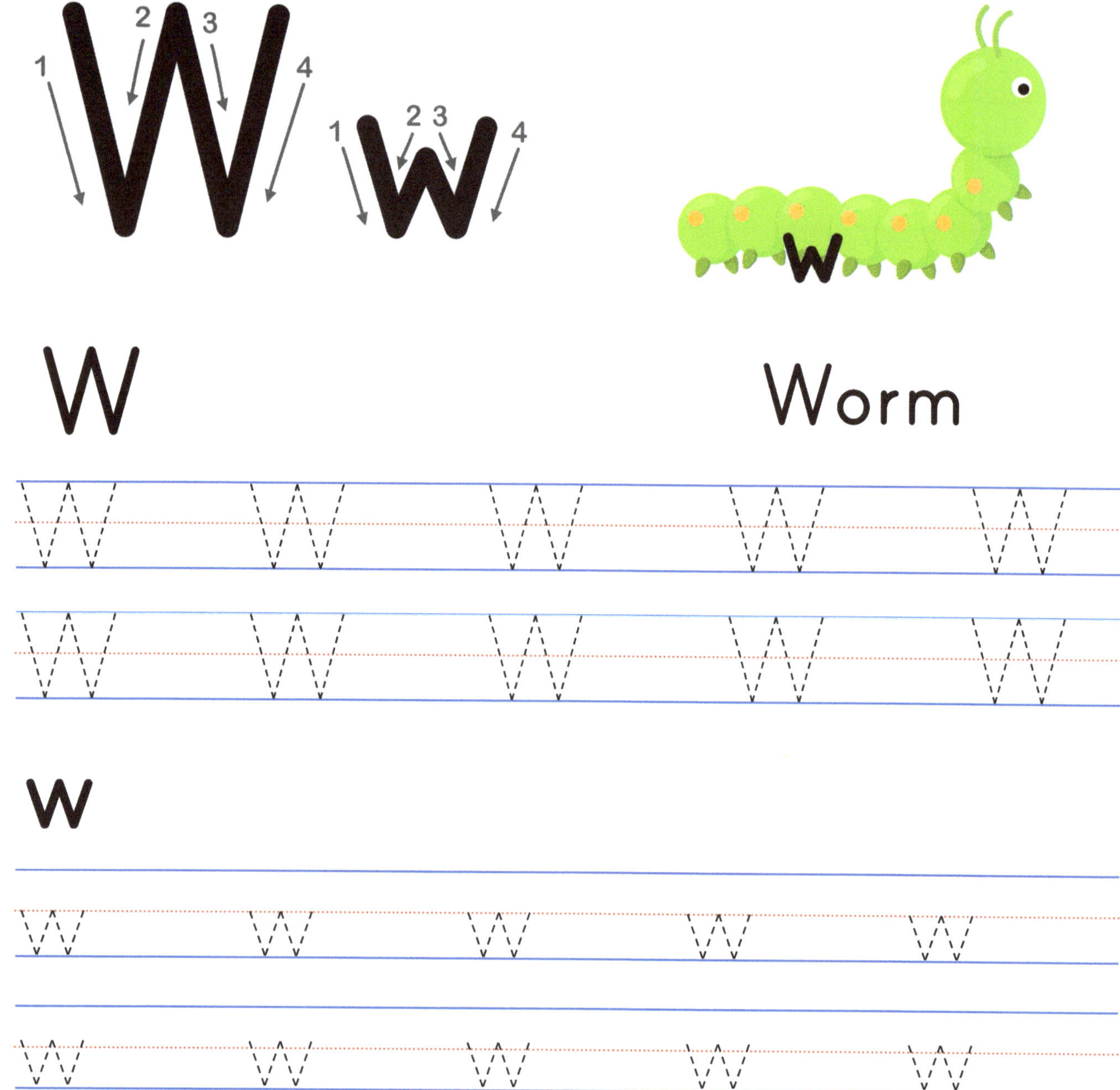

W

W

Worm

W

w

Trace the following uppercase and lowercase letters.

X

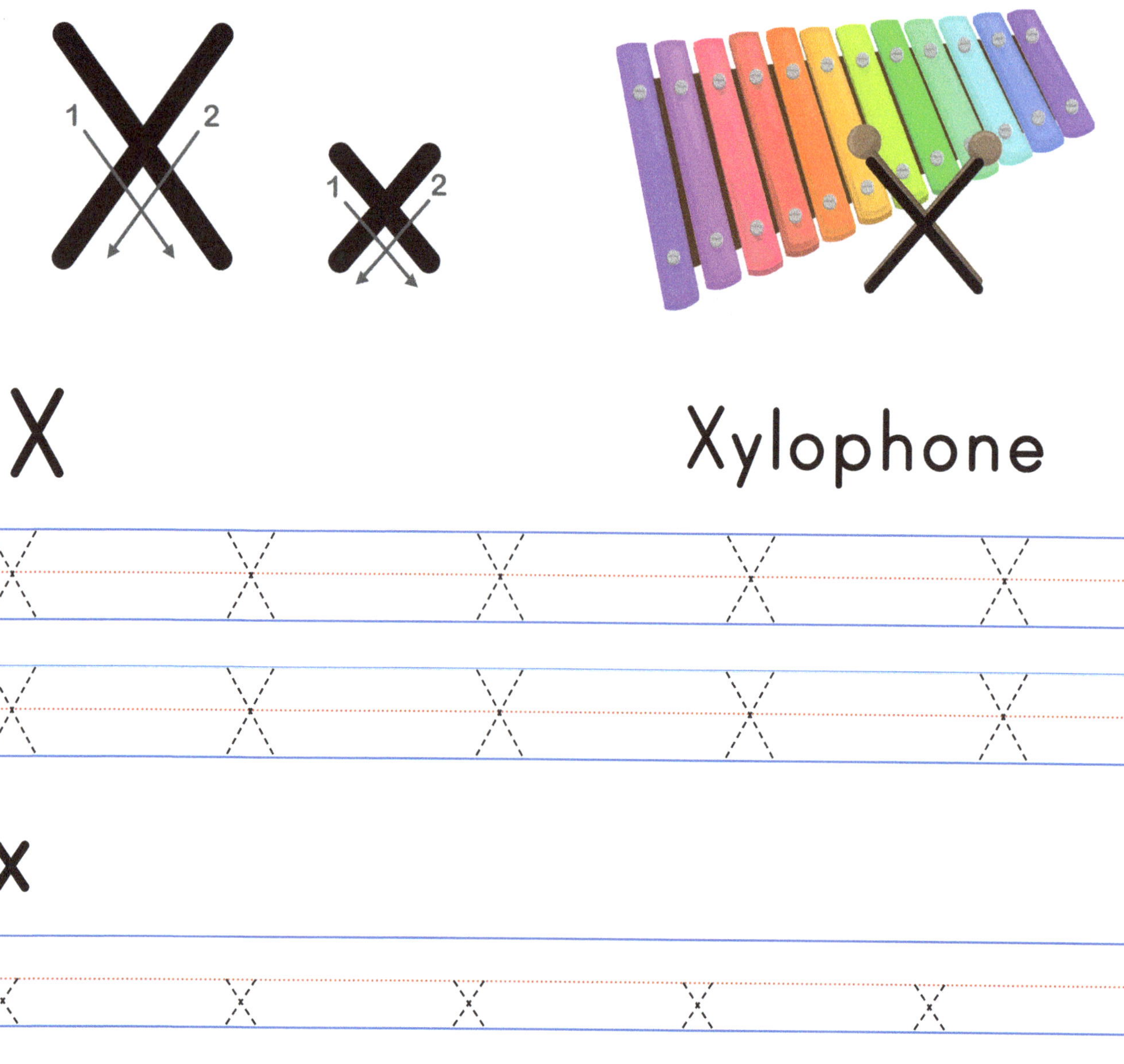

Xylophone

x

Trace the following uppercase and lowercase letters.

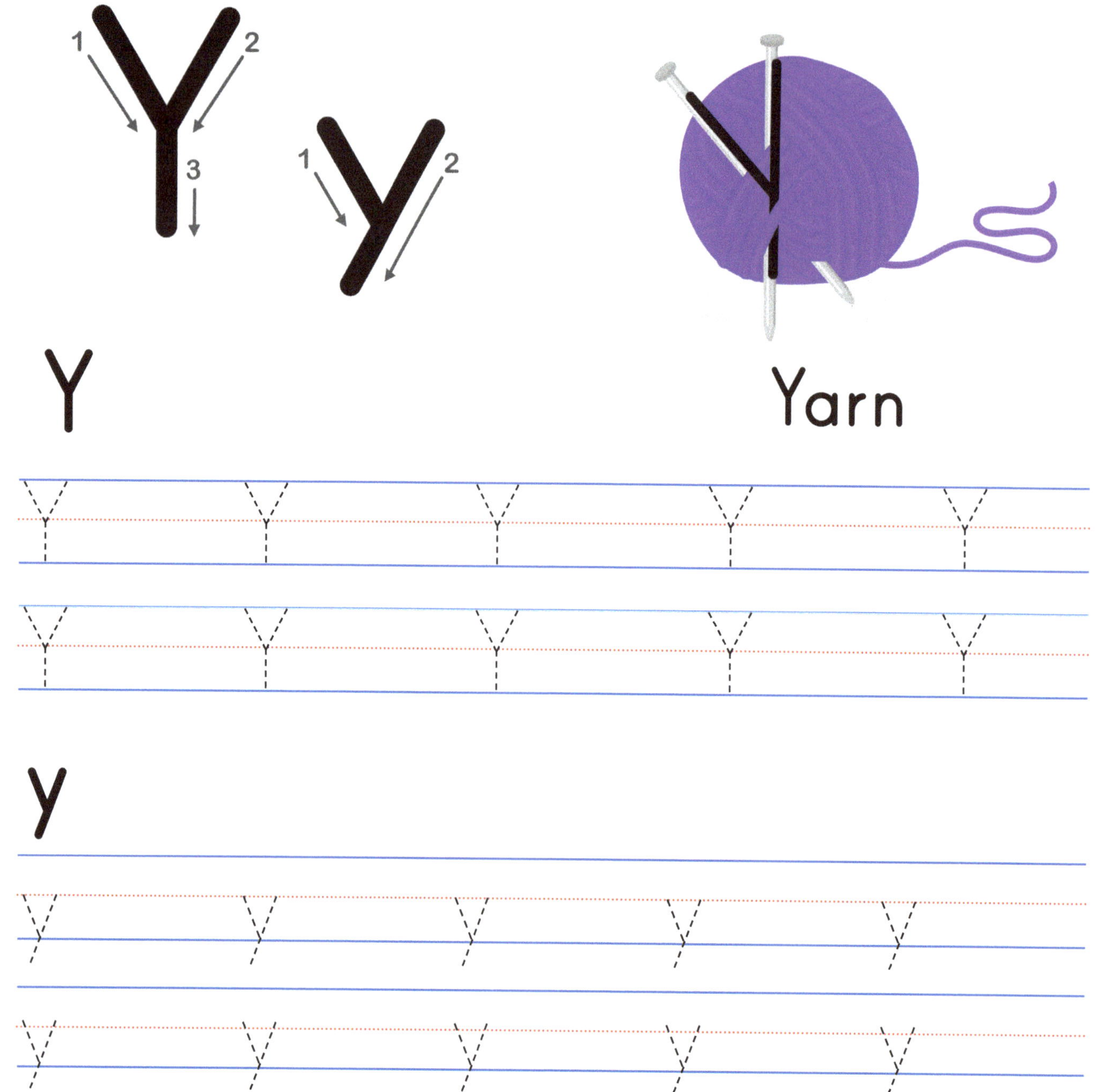

Y

Yarn

Y

y

Trace the following uppercase and lowercase letters.

Z

Zigzag

Trace the following uppercase and lowercase letters.

Write the missing uppercase letter

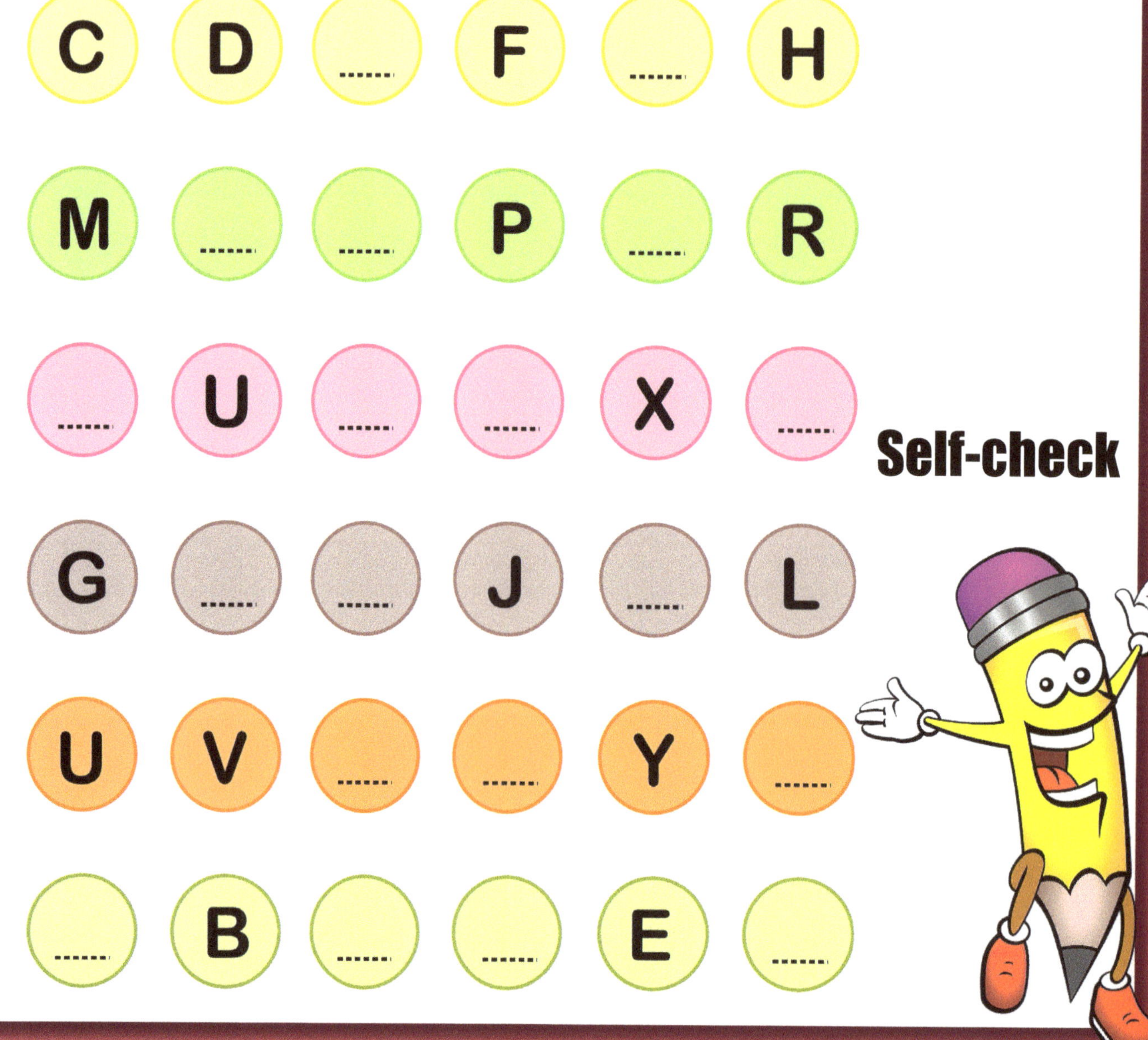

Self-check

Write the missing lowercase letter

c · d · ___ · f · ___ · h

m · ___ · ___ · p · ___ · r

___ · u · ___ · ___ · x · ___

g · ___ · ___ · j · ___ · l

u · v · ___ · ___ · y · ___

___ · b · ___ · ___ · e · ___

Self-check

Visit

www.BabyProfessorBooks.com

to download Free Baby Professor eBooks
and view our catalog of new and exciting
Children's Books